DATE		
DEC 0 9 2007		
JAN 1 2 2008		
FEB 0 6 2008		
FEB 2 8 2008		
JUL 1 6 2008		

Beginning to END

Cane To Sugar

A Buddy Book

by

Julie Murray

ABDO
Publishing Company

VISIT US AT
www.abdopublishing.com

Published by ABDO Publishing Company, 4940 Viking Drive, Edina, Minnesota 55435.

Copyright © 2007 by Abdo Consulting Group, Inc. International copyrights reserved in all countries. No part of this book may be reproduced in any form without written permission from the publisher. Buddy Books™ is a trademark and logo of ABDO Publishing Company.

Printed in the United States.

Coordinating Series Editor: Sarah Tieck
Contributing Editor: Michael P. Goecke
Graphic Design: Maria Hosley
Cover Photograph: Media Bakery, Photos.com
Interior Photographs/Illustrations: Photodisc, Photos.com
Special thanks to Maryborough Sugar Factory LTD in Queensland, Australia, and to U.S. Sugar Corp. in Florida for providing many of the interior photographs.

Library of Congress Cataloging-in-Publication Data

Murray, Julie, 1969–
    Cane to sugar / Julie Murray.
        p. cm. — (Beginning to end)
    Includes index.
    ISBN-13: 978-1-59679-834-2
    ISBN-10: 1-59679-834-3
    1. Sugar—Juvenile literature. 2. Sugar—Manufacture and refining—Juvenile literature. I. Title.

TX560.S9M87 2006
664'.122—dc22
                                                                2006019907

Table Of Contents

Where Does Sugar Come From?

Sugar has many uses. Many people use it to sweeten foods. They sprinkle sugar on cereal and grapefruit and pour it into coffee and other drinks.

Sugar is also an important **ingredient**. It is used in recipes for treats such as cakes and cookies. Do you know where sugar comes from?

Sometimes, people use sugar to sweeten fruits, such as blackberries and raspberries.

5

A Starting Point

Sugar is a natural product. It comes from a plant called sugar cane. This plant is a type of grass.

Sugar cane plants grow in **tropical climates**. They have thick stems. The stems are processed to be made into sugar **crystals**.

After farmers plant sugar cane (top), they water the crops (bottom).

FUN Facts
Did you know...

... Not all white sugar is made from sugar cane. Some sugar is made from beets.

... There are 15 calories in one teaspoon of sugar.

... Even though lemons taste sour, they contain sugar.

Penicillin

... Sugar does more than just make things taste sweet. It is also used to tan leather, grow penicillin, and make ink for printers.

The Beginnings Of Sugar

Before sugar can be made, farmers must first harvest the sugar cane stems. Workers cut the stems down. But, they are careful to leave roots. This way, the sugar cane can grow back.

After the cane is gathered, it is taken to a factory by truck or cart. At the factory, the cane is **manufactured** into sugar.

Sometimes, workers use machines to harvest sugar cane (top). Trucks take the harvested sugar cane to factories (bottom left) where it is unloaded (bottom right).

The Maryborough Sugar Factory is in Australia.

After the sugar cane arrives at a factory, it is smashed between large rollers. This helps remove sugary liquid from the stem.

Next, water is added to rinse more sugar from the cane. This mixture is called cane juice. Cane juice is the beginning of sugar.

12

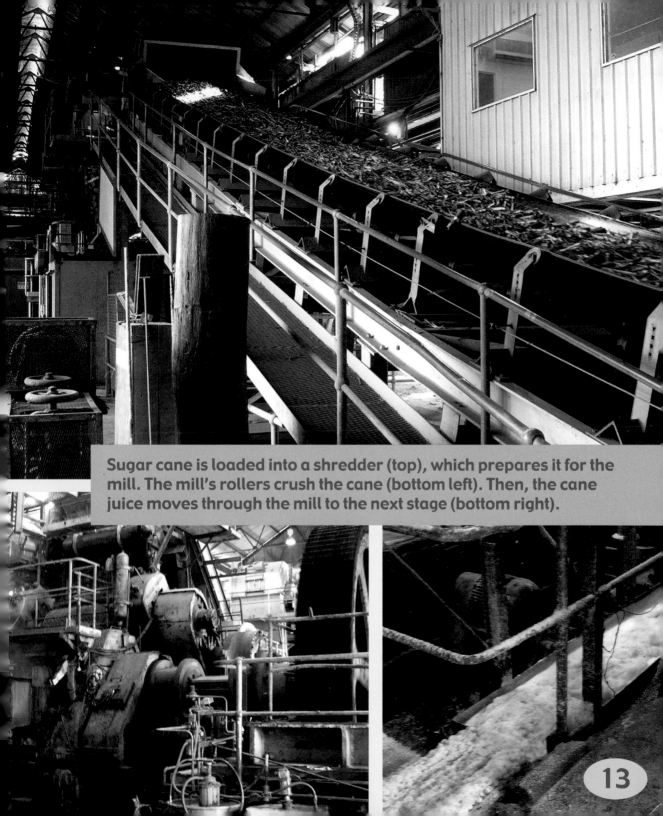

Sugar cane is loaded into a shredder (top), which prepares it for the mill. The mill's rollers crush the cane (bottom left). Then, the cane juice moves through the mill to the next stage (bottom right).

The Makings Of
Sugar

The cane juice needs to be cleaned. Factory workers add a **substance** to help remove dirt.

The next stage is called **evaporation**. During evaporation, the cane juice is boiled until it becomes syrup.

The juice heater (top left), the juice clarifier (top right), and the evaporator (bottom) are part of the production process at a sugar cane factory.

The cane syrup is very thick. Workers pour it into a large pan. Then, the syrup is boiled in a vacuum. The vacuum keeps it from burning.

At this stage, raw sugar **crystals** begin to form. Next, syrup is put into a spinning machine. This machine removes the extra liquid.

Crystals take a while to form from the thick syrup.

After crystals are formed in the pan stage (top), they spin in a centrifuge machine (bottom).

From Cane To Crystals

At first, raw sugar **crystals** are brown or yellow. Then, the raw sugar is **refined** even more. This process turns the sugar white.

After the sugar becomes white, it is packaged and sent to stores. People buy sugar to use for baking, mixing, and eating.

Raw sugar is piled at the factory (top left) before it is transported (top right). Then, the raw sugar is taken from the factory to a refinery for cleaning and packaging. The U.S. Sugar Refinery is in Florida (bottom).

Sugar is packaged in boxes to be taken to stores.

Sugar comes a long way from a sugar cane plant to sugar **crystals**. The next time you sprinkle sugar on your food, think about its journey!

Sugar crystals are visible on many candies.

Can You Guess?

Q: How many **crystals** are in one cube of sugar?

A: About 725,000!

Q: When were cartons first used to store sugar instead of wooden barrels?

A: 1899.

Important Words

climate the weather and temperatures that are normal in a certain place.

crystal a very small piece.

evaporate to change from a liquid into a gas.

ingredient a part of a mixture.

manufacture to make.

refine to remove parts that aren't wanted.

substance a material that occupies space.

tropical parts of the world where temperatures are warm and the air is moist all the time.

Web Sites

To learn more, visit ABDO Publishing Company on the World Wide Web. Web site links about this topic are featured on our Book Links page. These links are routinely monitored and updated to provide the most current information available.

www.abdopublishing.com

Index